Scotland Travel Guide

Thomas Leon

Scotland Travel Guide

ISBN-13: 978-1976445255
ISBN-10: 1976445256

First Edition: September 2017
10 9 8 7 6 5 4 3 2 1

Thomas Leon

CONTENTS

Introduction

Rugged, feisty and colorful, Scotland is also a world rich in culture and heritage that will undoubtedly take your senses on an adventure of their own.

Whether it's the rich and diverse culinary appeal—don't knock haggis 'til you've tried it—or the vibrant nightlife that gained Edinburgh notoriety all over the world, rest assured that you're in for the trip of a lifetime.

A seasoned globe-trotter, I've been through my share of adventures all over the world. But nothing could have prepared me for the stark beauty and vivid greenery that would greet me the minute I set foot in Scotland.

In this book, I aim to use my extensive travel experience to offer you insider tips to help you find the very best accommodation, restaurants and souvenirs according to your budget and personal preferences.

I'll also take you through the best-kept secrets in Scotland, enabling you to avoid heavy tourist areas and crowded places.

Join me in my quest to spot the elusive Loch Ness monster...

Hike with me across the stormy Highlands...

Let's explore centuries-old ruins and go bus-hopping across the entire country...

The one thing that really struck me in Scotland was the warm and festive culture that just envelopes you the moment you set foot in the country. Over the course of my travels, I have encountered very few countries that managed to replicate the genuine air of hospitality that the Scots exude.

I found that visiting Scotland was quite a sensory experience as well. The earthiness, the rugged landscape, the delectable array of local dishes and drinks, the billowing winds and the calm lochs all combine to make for an exceptionally pleasant assault on the senses.

Boasting an array of festivals and Celtic legends, Scotland did not fail to mesmerize me as I went on an expedition to explore some of the country's most ancient sites, most of which are of unknown origins. Believe me when I say that the history only serves to enhance the glorious mystique shrouding Scotland.

Without a doubt, it's a massive country and the sheer number of places to visit can be overwhelming for first-time travelers. Fret thee not, for in this book, I have complied an array of routes that will help you see the very best of Scotland. Whether you want a quiet, toned-down holiday, or a more eclectic one, rest assured that this culturally-rich country will have something for you.

You will find the best value for your money as I share my personal experiences. Whether you've already booked your trip or you're still debating, this book can guide you through some of the most spectacular Scottish attractions guaranteed to provide cherished memories long after you've headed back home.

So, grab your hiking boots, your sense of adventure, your best camera and this book and I'll take you across one of the best travel destinations of the world.

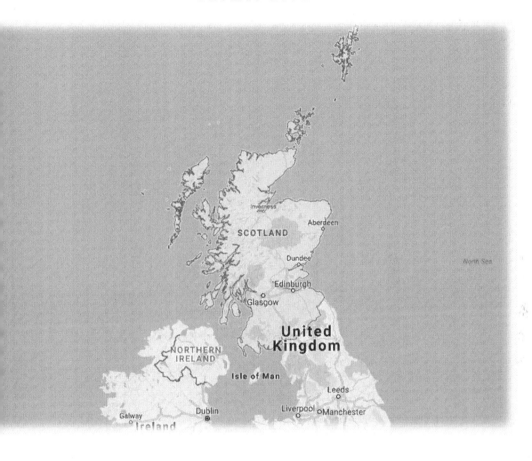

Chapter 1: Practical Information

Due to a diverse cultural heritage, Scotland does differ from other European countries in terms of cost, accommodation and food. If you've never visited this country before, there are a few things that you need to bear in mind prior to packing your bags.

So, before we dive into the best places to visit, here is some practical information you may want to get acquainted with before heading off to Scotland.

General costs

If you're not careful managing costs, Scotland can be on the expensive side. Accommodations, food and travel expenses all tend to be slightly higher than most prices in other European countries. The good news is that there are plenty of ways that can help you save money in Scotland. If you're travelling on a restricted budget, for example, it's best to favor hostels or B & B's, which can cost around £50 per day. I personally like to stay in smaller-scale family establishments where I can really drink in an authentic Scottish atmosphere punctuated by traditional meals.

In terms of costs, I would also strongly advise that you rent your own car if you're spending more than two weeks in Scotland. To save money, skip the fancy restaurants and opt instead for budget-friendly diners and pubs. Not only will this drastically reduce your expenses, but you'll also get to sample typical Scottish dishes with none of the commercial twists

What you should pack

Don't forget to grab a couple of sweaters, even if you're visiting in the summer. Indeed, the Scottish Highlands can get quite chilly, especially at night. The further up north you move, the colder it's going to get.

This country is also prone to windy and rainy spells, so it's always a good idea to invest in a solid pair of waterproof hiking shoes, especially if you're planning on doing a lot of walking. The rule of thumb in Scotland is to always be prepared. It's never a bad idea to keep an umbrella and waterproof coat at hand, even in the summer.

Getting around

As I mentioned earlier, I personally prefer to rent my own car when I'm visiting Scotland.

Of course, if you book a package tour, you won't have to worry about transportation. You'll find that most of the coach, bus and train stations are in Eastern and Central Scotland.

In fact, you'll find there are very few scheduled coaches or buses that cover the Southern Uplands or Western Highlands, so it's best to go around in your own car or book a cab for these regions.

If you are planning on renting a car, don't forget that they drive on the left side of the road in Scotland. Cars with automatic transmissions are more expensive than sticks, but you can get a good deal if you rent for a week or more.

Eating out in Scotland

There's nothing quite like Scottish food and the good news is that food is among the least expensive things in Scotland. Do arm yourself with plenty of appetite and—more importantly—your sense of adventure.

Their national dish is Haggis, which is basically a savory meat pudding cooked in a sheep's stomach. Yes, it sounds strange, I know. I had my reservations, too. But one bite and I was sold. There's something about the decadent meatiness and moistness that just lures you in and believe me when I say that there's nothing like a slice of haggis with onions, potatoes and oatmeal to cure last night's hangover. This dish is best sampled in a pub or a small-scale family restaurant.

Of course, there's no denying that you'll find your share of gourmet places to eat in Scotland. If you don't feel like unleashing your experimental taste buds yet, rest assured that the majority of eateries do offer both traditional European and American fare that might be closer to the type of food that you're used to.

Tipping

Like most European countries, tipping isn't necessarily expected in Scotland, but of course, it's appreciated.

In the case of a taxi, the norm is to tip around 10-12%, but an easier way is to simply round up the fare to a whole number. This same rule applies to restaurants, but bear in mind that it's not at all compulsory.

You will find that locals are quite generous when it comes to paying for your first drink at the pub, even if you're a complete stranger to them. It is customary to return the favor by paying for the second round.

Chapter 2: Exhilarating Scottish Adventures

If there is a country that can get your adrenaline

pumping, it's definitely Scotland. Scotsmen and women are known all over the world for their energetic demeanors and penchant for lively festivals and activities.

Should you want to take a page out of their books, here are some of the most exhilarating adventures to be experienced in Scotland.

10 of the best-kept secrets in Scotland

While Scotland is practically bursting with various attractions set to suit just about every preference, believe me when I say that most of the beauty of the country lies under the surface. Indeed, there are some regions of Scotland that are fiercely guarded by locals who want to protect these areas from mass tourism and commercialization. As a result, some of Scotland's most scenic places barely even appear in most brochures or websites.

To avoid wasting precious vacation time scuttling about Scotland in your quest to find those hidden gems, I would recommend simply drawing up a list of the lesser-known places you'd like to visit and ask your guide about them. Of course, it wouldn't hurt to get friendly with the locals either!

Here are 10 of my favorite, albeit lesser-known, Scottish attractions.

1. Torwood Blue Pool

Shrouded in mystery, Torwood Blue is a brick pool of

unknown origin that never fails to fascinate both locals and tourists alike. Located not far from Denny, this 4-meter deep pool once boasted a vivid blue hue, but has turned murky green thanks to years and years of algae growth. The mystique around this pool lies in the fact that even if the presence of brick walls indicates that it's entirely man-made, there are absolutely no signs as to why it was built, or who may have built it.

2. Ring of Brodgar

The lesser-known Scottish cousin of Stonehenge, the Ring of Brodgar forms part of the Heart of Neolithic Orkney World Heritage Site and is well-worth a visit if you're interested in historical architecture. According to historians, the Ring of Brodgar was created around 2500 BC and this place is yet another Scottish mystery since no one seems to know why it was even built.

3. Govanhill Baths

Known as the very last surviving bathhouse from the Edwardian era, Govanhill Baths is found in Glasgow. I have to admit I headed for this lesser-known attraction expecting something as grandiose as the Roman baths but I was surprised by the minimalist style and fairly sleek architecture. According to our guide, the Govanhill Baths now stands as a monument to what unity can achieve. Indeed, the council wanted to close the pool over a decade ago but locals staged a successful protest that lasted several years and ultimately, the community finally gained the bathhouse back. This establishment has three pools which were once used for bathing and washing clothes. Our guide also pointed out typically Edwardian features such as the sharp roof tilt and old-fashioned changing facilities which provided a stupendous slice of ancient culture.

4. Fairy Pool

Okay, take it from me, you absolutely need to check out the Fairy Pool if you're passing through Carbost, or if you're simply interested in Celtic Culture. According to local legend, this pool—which is made up of several small waterfalls—provides a secret hideaway for mystical creatures. Whether you believe the legend or not, rest assured that the crystalline waters provide the ideal swimming spot, especially in summer. For some reason, the waters always remain pleasurably cool, regardless of the weather, and this only serves to enhance the mystique that surrounds this hauntingly beautiful place.

5. Kilt Rock and Mealt Falls

This cluster of ancient cliffs is named so because they look surprisingly like a pleated kilt. If you stand on the Trotternish Peninsula viewpoint, you will be able to spot both the Kilt Rock cliffs and the Mealt waterfalls, which plummet spectacularly from the very top of the cliffs. Offering excellent photo opportunities, these two landmarks are also known for the haunting tone that emerges from the rocks whenever there's a strong wind.

6. Gilmerton Cove

In a small Edinburgh suburb known as Gilmerton, there was once a flourishing village. Nowadays, this village stands deserted, but historians have discovered a surprising series of passages and caves under the ground. Steer clear of the caves if you're claustrophobic. While it was undoubtedly a fascinating place to visit—and I would certainly visit it again, given the chance—one person from our group actually got sick because of the narrow passageways. If you don't have an issue with confined spaces, however, there's no doubt that this is one of the most fascinating places that you will ever visit.

7. The Royal Botanic Gardens of Edinburg

Hailed as one of the oldest and most diverse gardens in Europe, the Royal Botanic Gardens was first founded back in 1670, and while it was used primarily for medicinal plants at the time, this garden now displays 72 acres of varied plants and bushes. To me, this place literally felt like something out of a painting, with waterfalls, ponds, Victorian-style glasshouses and even pagodas on the Chinese hillside.

8. Eilean Donan

If you ask me, Eilean Donan is one of Scotland's most iconic—albeit lesser known—structures. With a rich history of residents and visitors, this castle is found not far from the sleepy Village of Dornie and is featured in its fair share of movies. If you ask me, the rugged building surrounded by vivid greenery, whistling wind and sharp peaks is what the Scottish wilderness is all about. While it offers excellent photo opportunities, we were quickly informed that drones are not allowed in this area. Regardless, it makes for quite an exhilarating hiking trip. Be sure to don waterproof shoes since this region is notoriously damp and muddy. And after the hike, you can warm up with a delectable mug of cocoa in the nearby café.

9. Fingal's Cave

Any doubt that Scotland is one of the most visually stunning places on earth is quickly dispelled by one trip to Fingal's Cave. According to our guide, this cave captivated its fair share of celebrities, including Pink Floyd and Jules Verne. And after seeing this place for myself, I can totally understand why. Made from perfectly hexagonal basalts naturally stacked on top of each other. Measuring 270 feet deep and 72 feet tall, this sea cave was once extremely popular among the ancient Celtic population in Scotland. Reminiscent of Ireland's Giant Causeway, Fingal's Cave is difficult to access unless you're an experienced hiker who's ready to escalade down the basalt columns. If not, you can always book a cruise where your boat will pass in front of the cave, proving you with an awe-inspiring glimpse of the mysterious interior.

10. Leighton Library

Yes I know. You didn't save up for a trip to Scotland to visit a library. At least that was my reaction when my Scottish friend dragged me over to Leighton Library. And boy, was I glad he did. This place may be small, unimpressive and ancient, but it was the very first library in Scotland and you can feel its history pressing down upon you the minute you enter the place. Under the library is a stone undercroft which once served to house the first Scottish librarians.

The Highlands Games

It's no secret that the Scots love to party. And there's no better way to get acquainted with the unique Scottish culture than to attend at least one of their festivals. In fact, because of the sheer number of festivals this country sees per year, there's a good chance that you'll get to attend one of them, regardless of when you visit.

You might have seen them in the movies, but here's your chance to see the Highlands Games from up-close. If you ask me, there's no better way than to combine Scottish and Celtic culture, community, and various forms of entertainment, all at the same time. Set against a spectacular backdrop, the Highlands Games often comprise of piping, field and track events, dance competitions, tug-o-war and of course, the world-famous caber toss, where participants literally lift up a humongous log with both hands and toss it as far and as high as they possibly can.

The Highlands Games are commonly held in summer and spring, and attract around 20,000 spectators every year. At the end of the games, we were even invited to an early Al-Fresco buffet dinner where everyone—participants, spectators, Scots and tourists alike—gathered over picnic tables for a jovial meal washed down with pints of whiskey and mulled wine.

Step onto the Royal Yacht

The world will not easily forget the one time that Queen Elizabeth's notoriously stiff upper lip finally gave way as she wept openly at the decommissioning ceremony of her royal yacht Britannia. Indeed, this yacht basically served as the royal family's floating holiday home for several decades and it is now permanently moored in the Ocean Terminal in Edinburgh. Because the yacht is now open to the public, you'll get to visit every nook and cranny of the yacht as you get acquainted with how the royal family used to live. Our guide told us that most of the décor was handpicked by Prince Phillip and Queen Elizabeth herself, so rest assured that you'll have an amazing insight into their personal tastes.

Our tour was assisted by an audio guide that can play up to 27 different languages and surprisingly enough, the ticket was only around £15.50 per person. Rest assured that the tour moves at your own pace so you can always bring your kids or elderly relatives along. I have to say that I was quite surprised by Queen Elizabeth's unfussy décor, indeed, instead of the glitz and silk drapes that I was expecting, I was greeted by quite a sophisticated interior, done up in muted and earthy hues. Still, you do spot the occasional royal indulgence here and there, like the thermometer installed in the bathroom to ensure that the Queen's bathwater was always up to optimal temperature.

On the yacht, you'll also find the Royal Deck Tea Room where you can enjoy a spot of Scottish-style afternoon tea, just like the royal family used to. We visited the Britannia near the end of autumn and believe me when I say that I've never appreciated the gloriously warm comfort of a perfectly brewed pot of tea so much before! Of course, in true Scottish fashion, you can easily substitute your cup of tea for a tall glass of malted whisky, or even a flute of champagne. Sandwiches, soups, cakes and scones are also available. At the end of the tour, you can also check out the gift shop and load up on official Britannia souvenirs that include glassware, china, and plush toys, as well as different types of accessories and jewelry.

Standing Stones of Callanish

If you like England's Stonehenge, you'll undoubtedly love the Standing Stones of Callanish. You are allowed to move closer to the Scottish standing stones, as opposed to the English ones. These are also not as famous, which means you won't need to battle packed crowds of eager tourists. In fact, on the day that I visited the standing stones, there was no one there other than another group of five people, giving us the chance to really take in the raw beauty of this place.

Our guide informed us that the Standing Stones of Callanish were actually built in the Neolithic era and used to be a place of worship or ritual activity for the villagers during the Bronze Age. It's good to bear in mind that the locals have several legends to explain the origins of the stones; another story, for example, states that the formations are actually giants that were turned to stone by a fanatical priest. And according to some locals that we met on the way, a deity known as 'The Shining One' walks between the stones every midsummer morning.

Regardless of whether you believe the local legends or not, there's no denying that the Standing Stones of Callanish are well-worth a visit. Best of all, there's absolutely no entrance fee for independent visits. However, you can always book a tour, as our group did, during which a guide will also take you across to the neighboring attractions such as the Isle of Harris and the Isle of Lewis. Not far from the Standing Stones is the Calanais Centre where you'll find a café, a gift shop and even an exhibition entitled 'The Story of the Stones.'

Sea Kayaking the Knoydart Peninsula

Located on the Western coast, this remote Peninsula is one of the most isolated areas in Scotland. And when I say isolated, I do mean isolated. There is absolutely no road access to the peninsula, so the only way to access it is by boat. We did decide to take our adventure up a notch though and kayak all the way there. This is quite a popular adventure in Scotland, so get ready to see dozens of small kayaks bobbing across the water next to you.

Boasting a mountainous and wild interior, the Knoydart Peninsula is the perfect place to escape if you want to enjoy some respite from your everyday life. Most companies offer guided day trips or bespoke expeditions on the peninsula, complete with lunch and snacks. A word of caution if you decide to book a kayaking experience though. As calm and inviting as the waters look, there is quite a bit of current which means you'll need to be in fairly good physical shape if you want to make it all the way to Knoydart. It actually took us slightly over three hours to reach our destination, by the end of which our arms were quite sore.

Still, I can say with absolute certainty that all the paddling and rowing was absolutely worth it! Scotland does have several isolated regions, but the Knoydart Peninsula felt like a whole other country altogether. If you want to spend some time on the peninsula, you can check out the Knoydart House which offers luxury accommodation right in this remote stretch of land.

Chapter 3: Popular Scottish Attractions

These are the attractions that helped make Scotland one of the prime tourist destinations in the world. If you're visiting during peak season, I would recommend that you make your reservations well in advance to ensure that you're able to actually get a booking. There might be some crowds as well but I found that getting an early start to the day actually helped avoid long lines and endless waits. Bear in mind that in several cases, booking online can actually be cheaper than on-site booking.

With all that in mind, let's move on to some of the most popular attractions in Scotland.

Try to spot the Loch Ness Monster

I visited the Loch Ness as part of a £42 tour of the Scottish Highlands and yes, we did spend a fair amount of time trying to spot the infamous monster, unsuccessfully, by the way. A friend even held a pair of binoculars in one hand and a camera in the other, so convinced that Nessie was finally going to gratify us with an appearance.

Of course, this didn't happen but regardless, there's no denying that the Loch Ness experience is exceptionally thrilling. I would strongly suggest that you book a cruise across the lake if you're a bit of a daredevil. Whether you believe that Nessie exists or not, it's always at the back of your head that a massive monster could jump up at any second, and this only serves to add to the special thrill that our cruise brought. One tip that our boat steward gave us was to look out for circles of disturbed water which, according to him meant that Nessie was close.

Reputed for its glorious scenery, this iconic lake is known as one of the deepest in Europe, with banks that plunge down to over 800 feet. Nearby, you'll find the villages of Dores and Foyers, two regions that I highly recommend you visit if you've got the time to spare. Some companies also offer lunch cruises across the Loch Ness, so be sure to browse around for package options. Tours like the 'Original Loch Ness Tour' that we booked took us across other striking places in the nearby surroundings such as Forth Bridges, Highland Perthshire, Cairngorm National Park, Inverness, The Great Glen, Fort William, Glen Coe, Rannoch Moor and Callander. I would strongly suggest that you set aside a whole day for these adventures though, since there's just so much to do and explore in the area.

Scottish Whiskey Experience

Unless you're teetotaler or a recovering alcoholic, it would be absolutely unfathomable to visit Scotland and not book at least one whiskey tour. A more cost-effective option, however, would be to opt for a multi-distillery tour, enabling you to seamlessly combine boozy fun with breathtaking scenery.

Below are some of the most popular Scottish Whisky adventures in the country.

Head over to The Islay Malts for the best whiskey in the world

According to popular belief, Irish monks were the first to introduce whiskey to Scotland. The Islay Malts boast some of the more fertile soil in the world, providing the ideal conditions for growing barley. Bear in mind that the island can only be accessed by boat, but the scenery was truly spectacular. You'll find two main distilleries on the island—Laphroaig and Lagavulin—and according to our guide, Islay is rich in peat which explains the strong, aromatic flavor that made Islay Single Malt Whiskeys so popular all over the world.

Go to whiskey school with the Scotch Whiskey Experience

My personal favorite, the Scotch Whiskey Experience, offers different types of tours in their Edinburgh distillery. I booked the 'Taste of Scotland' tour, which includes a Platinum Tour of the distillery followed by a typical three-course Scottish lunch in the on-site restaurant. On top of the free shots we got to sample during our tour, we were also offered a free dram of whiskey with our dessert. Because it is one of the most popular whiskey tours in Scotland, it is highly advised to book in advance.

While the Scotch Whiskey Experience cost £70.00, this distillery also offers less costly options such as 'The Silver Tour,' 'The Platinum Tour, 'The Gold Tour' and the 'Morning Masterclass'. If you're an absolute whiskey enthusiast, I would suggest that you book the masterclass which includes an exclusive viewing of some of the most famous Scotch whiskies in the world, as well as a mini-course in making whiskey, where you will learn about nosing, comparative testing and sensory perception tests. Best of all? You'll get to head home with a boxed crystal whiskey tasting glass, several miniature samples and even a complimentary gift.

Sample luxury whiskey at the Strathisla Distillery, Banffshire

Known as the oldest distillery in the Scottish Highlands, the Strathisla distillery is set on one of the most stunning terrains in Scotland. Set on the banks of the Isla River, and surrounded by picturesque buildings, this distillery even comes with its own cobbled courtyard and pagodas. Built in1786, the company was acquired by the Chivas Brothers back in 1950, giving rise to the world-famous Chivas Regal. If you want to skip the tour and settle down with samples instead (as I did, but don't judge!), you can go for the 'Chivas Cellar Tasting' where you'll get to sip on various types of whiskey straight from the massive casks. We got to some Chivas Ultis as well as 12, 18 and 25-year old Chivas Regal.

Experience the thrill of the Scottish Highlands

If you're looking for the kind of blissful solitude that will make you forget there's actually a modern civilization out there, consider this. With wonderfully shaped mountain ranges, wildlife, rugged coastlines and of course, more castles than you dare imagine, the Scottish Highlands are picturesque enough to have featured in some major blockbuster movies such as the Harry Potter series. Filled with mystique and the kind of scenery that you can only expect to see on the back of a postcard, the Scottish Highlands do offer plenty of exhilarating activities, such as these.

Guided Walks

The air in the Scottish Highlands is quite unlike anything I've ever experienced before. Indeed, the surrounding mountain ranges and the lack of city pollution make for a refreshing and highly invigorating walk. The good news is that guided walks are extremely popular tourist attractions in the Highlands, so you can be sure to find one that matches your budget and expectation. Be ready to set aside an entire day for the guided walk, and don't forget to bring your umbrella as well as a pair of waterproof boots, even if you're visiting during summer.

Now, if you're an avid hiker, you might want to book a week-long or even a 2-week guided walk that will take you across some of Scotland's most remote—and stunning—regions. The Big Highland Tour, for example, is offered by Walkabout Scotland and takes you across a 2 week hiking trip, where you will spend your days trekking across the Highlands. Accommodation is arranged in small hotels, guest houses and B & B's, and you will get to visit iconic places such as Coire Mhic Fhearchair, Coire Lagan, Boreraig and Suisnish, Ben Lomond as well as Ben A'an and The Trossachs, among others.

Mountain biking with a Scottish picnic

In case you don't know already, Scotland has a reputation as one of the best destinations for mountain biking. If you're an avid biker, rest assured that the Highlands offer the perfect setting to get your adrenaline pumping. Out of the numerous downhill sites dedicated to mountain biking in the Highlands, we opted for Laggan Wolftrax. The best thing about this particular track is that it literally offers various types of terrains to suit different levels of fitness. Laggan Wolftrax also features a café that you'll certainly be most grateful for at the end of the adventure!

Now, if you're not sure which trail is best suited for you, the center enables visitors to test out the different terrains through the skill loops found at the trailhead. The most popular trails for mountain biking are listed here.

- 3.6km Orange/Bike Park

- 6.4km Black Trail

- 15.2km Red Trail

- 4.8km Green Trail

The Harry Potter Experience

Whether you're a fan of Harry Potter or not, there is no denying that the movies were filmed in some of the most striking locations of Scotland, and are well-worth a visit. Best of all, Harry Potter adventures are quite popular in the country, so it will be extremely easy for you to find various types of packages offering trips to the major filming locations.

Personally, I can absolutely recommend a train trip across the Glenfinnan Viaduct railway in Lochaber. This Victorian railway will undoubtedly take your breath away as it zips across the countryside where mountains, lakes and wild forests blend seamlessly. This is the exact same bridge that was portrayed in the second and third movie as the Hogwarts Express roared towards Hogwarts.

Of course, if you're an avid fan of the book or the movie series, you'll definitely want to visit the now-famous Elephant House café. This is where J.K. Rowling first started writing the books, way back when she was still a broke and struggling single mother trying to provide for her infant child. According to urban legends, the author sought refuge in the café when it got too cold for her flat since she couldn't afford heating. Whether this anecdote is real or not remains to be seen, but there is no denying that the Elephant House café is the 'birth place' of the Harry Potter series and has become something of a pilgrimage for hardened fans. In fact, the table by the window where she used to write is always in high demand, so be sure to book early. As a bonus point, this café serves up some delectable coffee and the best scones I've ever had in Europe!

Other locations that feature in the movies include—but are by no means limited to—Rannoch Moor in Lochaber, Loch Etive in Argyll and Bute, Glen Coe in Highland, Black Rock Gorge in Ross and Cromarty, and Steall Falls, among others. It should still be noted that the train across the Glenfinnan Viaduct railway doesn't run every day, so I would suggest that you book in advance.

Scottish Bus Tours

There is no easier and cheaper way to drink in as much of Scotland in just a few days than to book a bus tour. Not unlike those double-decker buses that you often see zooming around London, Scottish bus tours often span across several days, offering you the chance to see the kind of remote places that might have cost you significantly more to visit on an independent trip.

Below are a couple of the highest-rated bus tours in Scotland:

Whiskey Tour of Scotland

This particular bus tour departs from Inverness and ends in Glasgow. One of the most in-depth whiskey tours in Scotland, this particular trip spans across an entire week and only accommodates 24 people per trip, which guarantees a personalized guide and service. Ideal for those who want to get acquainted with Scottish culture, this tour also offers you the chance to taste over 120 varieties of whiskey. Visitors will get to check out the Dalmore, Glenmorangie, Glengoyne, Ben Nevis and Talisker distilleries. Meals and accommodation are arranged.

Best of Scotland Coach Tour

If you want to visit both the Isle of Sky and the Scottish Highlands in the same trip, this is the tour for you. With a maximum group size of 45, this tour drives you across the Glengoyne whiskey distillery, Trossachs National Park, Scottish Highlands and the Isle of Skye. This trip not only includes meals and accommodation, but also luxury transfers in an air-conditioned coach with WiFi, audio headsets, city tours and plenty of photo opportunities.

The Scottish Isles

Believe it or not, Scotland has more than 790 tiny islands to its name, most of which are separated into different groups, mainly: Outer Hebrides, Inner Hebrides, Orkney, Shetland, Solway Fifth, Firth of Forth and the Firth of Clyde. Of course, there is no way to visit all these islands in one single trip, and probably not even in several trips!. But if you do get the chance to check out at least a few of them, rest assured that you will be exposed to Scotland's multi-cultural aspect that lies in its English, Nordic and Celtic history. Whether you've got a few days or a few weeks to spare, the easiest way to go island hopping in Scotland is by booking a pre-existing or tailor-made package to avoid having to book individual cruises and tours. Here are a few of the islands that I visited:

Isle of Bute

With scenic vistas and a plethora of relaxing paths to explore, there is no denying that the Isle of Bute is ideal for anyone who wants to experience the Scottish wilderness at its rawest. I was quite stunned by the gloriously preserved Victorian architecture that dots Rothesay, the main town. With a station, ferry service and old-fashioned buildings, there's an undeniable sense of nostalgia and old-school charm about the place that only serves to emphasize the overall sense of relaxation. This isle does come with a hotel, should you wish to spend the night.

In spite of its diminutive size, I was pleasantly surprised to see that the Isle of Bute has its fair share of architectural attractions. From century-old chapels to ruins of various kinds or even the world-famous Mount Stuart House, be ready to feast your eyes on a thrilling display of neo-gothic architecture.

Isle of Skye

If you want to enjoy a romantic evening under the stars, this is the place to go. A tiny islet brimming with magnetic mountains, acres of greenery and a wonderfully mystical atmosphere, the Isle of Skye is one of Scotland's most popular islets, and for good reason. As one of the largest Scottish isles, you'll be able to enjoy a wide range of attractions from pony trekking to craft shops. A personal recommendation of mine would be the Talisker Distillery located at Carbost. Not only is this among the oldest working distillery in Scotland, but you also get to sample some of their best products at the end of the tour. Prices vary between £10 and £40, depending on the type of tour that you've booked.

Getting to the Isle of Skye is quite easy. From the West coast of Scotland, you can either take the ferry from Mallaig or Glenelg, or drive across the bridge from Kyle of Lochalsh. In fact, if you do decide to take the Kyle of Lochalsh route, which I can absolutely recommend, you can even check out the Eilean Donan Castle on the way. This 13th century old building is extremely popular among tourists and locals alike, and you can almost feel the history of the place weighing upon you as you walk in. Do check the opening hours though since they vary according to seasons.

Shetland

This is the one place you absolutely have to check out if you want to unleash your adventurous bone. Shetland is actually an archipelago that is comprised of over 1000 islands, some of which are inhabited. Admittedly, this archipelago is closer to Norway than Scotland, but it does fall under Scottish territory. What I liked the most about Shetland was its unique Scandinavian heritage, reflected in the local dialect. With over 6000 years of history to its name, this archipelago is brimming with perfectly-preserved ruins, archeological sites, standing stones that date all the way back to the Iron Age, croft-houses and even Pictish wheelhouses. Offering the perfect glimpse into Shetland's vivid history, the small, picturesque towns are fringed with moorlands, beaches and clifftops that were formed after centuries and millennia of weathering. Some of my favorite Shetland attractions include Jarlshof, the Hermaness Nature Reserve, Shetland Museum and the Isle of Noss, which forms part of the archipelago.

Chapter 4: Eating in Scotland

Take it from me, eating in Scotland is quite unlike anything else. Nothing could have prepared me—or my taste buds for that matter—for the exceptional fusion of flavors that greeted me when I sampled Scottish food for the first time. Be warned though, some Scottish delicacies are an acquired treat and some might be completely off-putting. Still, if you dare, I would strongly suggest that you venture out of your comfort zone and give the more dubious-looking delicacies a nibble.

Who knows? You might just end up polishing off the entire plate!

What to expect

The rich Scottish heritage is very often reflected in its culinary treats. Indeed, freshness is always the key in Scotland and one rarely finds any overly-processed ingredient in their food. With a vast and exotic wildlife, there's no doubt that you can enjoy plenty of fresh seafood, meat and chicken, all washed down with pints of lager or whiskey. There was something about the deep earthiness of Scottish food that never failed to captivate me, regardless of whether I ate in local pubs or more refined restaurants.

Still, if you're under the impression that Scots are health nuts, think again. This is, after all, the country that invented the deep fried Mars bar, so do think about packing those pants with elastic waistbands before heading off to Scotland! As far as fast food is concerned, you'll certainly find your share of McDonalds and the likes in the main cities, such as Glasgow and Edinburgh, but people living in remote regions and the Highlands tend to favor healthier, home-cooked meals.

Here are some of the most popular Scottish foods:

- **Breakfast options:** Tea, yogurt, sausages, kippers, oatmeal, toast with butter and marmalade, baked beans, broiled tomatoes, bacons, potato patties, sautéed mushrooms, black pudding, white pudding and eggs.

- **Lunch options:** Sandwiches with various fillings, hearty meat and vegetable soup, steak pie with a side of chips, fish and chips, baked potatoes (called jacket potatoes) with different toppings.

- **High tea options:** Tea or coffee, fresh tomato slices, slices of coconut cake with strawberry jam, scones and clotted cream, finger sandwiches, small pancakes (called crumpets), slices of toast with butter and marmalade.

- **Dinner options** (also referred to as tea or supper): Haggis with mashed potatoes and roast root vegetables; stovies, which is basically beef with fried onions and potatoes served with beetroot and oatcakes; smoked haddock served with onions and potatoes; and venison steak with roast potatoes.

- **Dessert options:** Deep-fried mars bar, fruity gingerbread, Scotch teas, apple shortbread pie, toffee pudding, oat cakes, orange and chocolate mousse with whisky, berry brulee, raspberry buns, whiskey tablet fudge, Scottish shortbread.

Meal times and costs

Not unlike Britain, meal times in Scotland can be rather inflexible, especially if you're staying in an inn or a hotel where kitchens most certainly close on time. The hotel where I stayed when I was in Glasgow, for example, only served breakfast until 9am. Lunch was from noon to 2pm, and while my hotel didn't serve the traditional afternoon tea, most establishments do dedicate 3-4pm to the traditional Scottish High Tea. Dinner ran from 6 to 9pm, but bear in mind that some places can close as early as 8pm, especially on weekdays. The majority of establishments— especially pubs—are much more flexible on Friday nights.

As far as the costs are concerned, most supermarket sandwiches and drinks cost you around £4-6. Dinner at a small-scale, family-owned pub costs around £10-£20 per person with drinks included, while a fancy restaurant might set you back around £30-40 per person, including wine.

With all that in mind, let's move on to some of the best places to eat in Scotland.

The Pub Experience

Ingrained in Scottish culture, pubs are absolute landmarks in the country, not unlike its multitude of castles and ruins. Best of all, pubs provide some of the most succulent and least expensive meals that you can get in Scotland. There is something about the convivial and hilariously rowdy atmosphere that does seem to echo the playful vibe that reigns in the country. Listed below are some of the best pubs that I visited in Glasgow and Edinburgh.

Edinburgh

With a phenomenal nightlife, Edinburgh is undoubtedly the place to be on a Friday night. One of the liveliest cities I've ever had the pleasure of visiting, it's not at all uncustomary to hear rhythmic beats escaping from pubs and restaurants as you walk down the streets at night. Here are just a few of my favorite pubs in Edinburgh.

The Café Royal

Okay, this one is not exactly cheap, I'll admit. And while I felt that this place had more of a bistro vibe to it, locals assured me that it is indeed a pub. The Café Royal may not have the same rustic atmosphere as the countryside pubs, but is the place to be if you want to experience a more refined slice of Scottish culture. With a Parisian-style saloon interior, this particular pub is extremely packed on the weekend. I went there on a Saturday afternoon and we did have to wait a while for a table, in spite of our reservations, but it was definitely worth the wait. In spite of its glitzy décor, the food was surprisingly earthy and rustic. If you're a fan of seafood, you'll be glad to learn that the pub also offers an oyster bar.

Bennets Bar

With a gloriously rustic décor enhanced by dark wood paneling, Bennets Bar is found in the heart of Edinburgh, right next to the King's Theatre. Boasting an electric vibe that's only enhanced by the cluster of locals, thespians, tourists and theatre-goers, this pub is apparently one of the oldest and most authentic establishments in Edinburgh. Since 1839, Bennets Bar is known not only for its excellent collection of whiskey, but also for its 'Bennets Burger' which is essentially made up of a thick, juicy cut of beef served on a brioche bun with beetroot relish and chips.

Sandy Bell's

With a frills-free décor, Sandy Bell's has always been popular among eccentric musicians and actors. The first thing that really struck me when I entered the place was the glorious whiskey-coffee scent that fused together to create a homey atmosphere. Because it is such a hit among musicians, rest assured that music strums through the night, even during weekdays. I have to admit that I was quite impressed by the pub's impressive collection of rare liquors and traditional Scottish whiskey that include Speyside, Highland, Island, Lowland, Islay, English, Campbeltown, Edinburgh, and even Japanese malt whiskey.

Glasgow

If you ask me, Glasgow is just as lively as Edinburgh, but while the capital offers a more modern approach to Scottish culture, this city retained quite a lot of its Gaelic ancestry. With a wide range of cultural activities that include pub crawling.

Waxy O'Connor

One of the most affordable pubs in Scotland, Waxy O'Connor is reputed for its vibrant atmosphere and home brews. Boasting a homely interior, this Scottish pub spreads over three floors, proving ample space in spite of the crowds. Trust me when I say this is the place to be if you want to experience a bona fide Scottish Friday night. Best of all, this pub serves some excellent food at a surprisingly low price and even on busy nights, your waiter won't hesitate before recommending the perfect drinks and food pairings.

Curler's Rest

Located in the West End, Curler's Rest oozes Scottish

hospitality and warmth, with plenty of merriment and good food on the menu. This was the place where I was able to really soak up an authentic Glasgow atmosphere. Featuring quirky charm and some of the juiciest burgers I've ever tasted, this pub also specializes in traditional Scottish Sunday Roasts which comprise of Yorkshire pudding, roasted pork, chicken or beef, fried or roasted potatoes, gingerbread stuffing, braised cabbage and gravy, among others. Drinks are extremely varied as well, with a particular focus on malt whiskey. Portion sizes are generous and well-worth the fairly affordable price tag.

The Laurieston

With an almost omnipresent Friday Night vibe—regardless of which day of the week it is—the Laurieston is nothing short of a landmark in Glasgow. I'll admit the rather frayed exterior and downtrodden building doesn't exactly scream welcome, and we did have our reservations about going in, but boy am I glad we did! Later, we found out that the structure is actually a nod to the 60's and this same nostalgic feel is beautifully replicated in the homey interior. In fact, the first impression that hit me when I stepped in was that this pub looked more like some kind of museum filled with exquisite antiquities. Everything was there from the small red tables to the circular bar, wooden floor and 60's style stools. And believe it or not, this place even has an old-fashioned pie machine filled with plump, juicy savory and sweet pies.

We only went there for drinks, so I can't exactly vouch for the food, though the locals I spoke to gave their dinner menu rave reviews. The drinks were exquisitely refreshing with pungent finishes that paired nicely with our bar snacks. Their pint of ice-cold Fosters was so spot on that I just had to have another. More importantly, the prices are quite reasonable, especially when compared to Edinburgh.

Fine Dining in Scotland

While it's not exactly reputed for it, Scotland does offer a variety of fine dining restaurants for you to choose from as well. Unlike commercialized restaurants, however, the great majority of the dishes had a distinctively homemade edge to them. Just be sure to have your wallets at the ready since unlike those Glasgow pubs, most gourmet restaurants were quite expensive, but well-worth the occasional indulgence!

Martin Wishart Restaurant

Set in Edinburgh, the Martin Wishart Restaurant was founded by the chef, Martin Wishart himself. While I didn't get to meet the chef in person, some local friends told me that he trained under renowned chefs such as Michel Roux Jr and Albert Roux. Featuring a sophisticated décor that reflects the quiet elegance of Edinburgh, this restaurant is reputed for the fresh and locally-grown produce that goes into its dishes. If you can't decide what to settle for, you can always go for the 6 or 8 course tasting menu, available in both vegetarian and non-vegetarian versions. An a la carte option is also included, which includes plenty of unique dishes such as the Tartare of Rose Veal, which is served with hazelnut oil and Oscietra caviar buttermilk.

Gordon's Restaurant

Located in Angus, Gordon's Restaurant is an absolute must-try if you're a fan of haute cuisine and—more importantly—of Chef Ramsay. What really surprised me (in a good way!) with this particular establishment is the fact that they even offer rooms above the restaurant where you can spend the night if you don't feel like driving back to your hotel, or if you've had too much to drink at dinner! Guests can choose from five different types of comfortable rooms that echo a classic Scottish décor with quilted bedding and Harlequin velvet.

Before we move on to the food, I have to quickly add that the wine list at Gordon's Restaurant was easily among the most extensive and varied that I've ever seen over the course of my travels. A sommelier is also on standby to help you find the very best pairings with your meals. Some of the most popular items on the menu include North Sea Turbot served with mushroom puree, crispy chicken wings and chargrilled sweetcorn, Angus Scotch Beef Fillet served with Rioja jus, Hay Baked Celeriac, Bacon Jam and Truffle Ravioli, as well as Isle of Skye scallops served with curry dressing, duck ham and pea puree.

The Manor House and Restaurant

Located in Oban, the Manor House Restaurant was actually established back in 1780 for the Duke of Argyll. This four-star establishment is especially focused on local produce, meats and seafood which bring a gloriously fresh and earthy taste to their dishes. While you can certainly find some quintessential Scottish meals on the menu, I was pleasantly surprised to see that they also serve some traditional French dishes. Our waiter informed us that all of the Manor House seafood is sourced from the nearby Donald Watt Fishmongers, where the fish is caught off the west coast of Scotland. As a result, the menu also features specialty seafood such as lobsters, crabs, monkfish, hake, halibut and langoustine.

Some of their signature dishes include the Hand Divided Scallop with Salmon Mousse and Lobster, Glazed Asparagus with Beetroot and Fried Egg, Scottish Fillet of Beef with Asparagus and Fondant Potato as well as Crispy Filo Tart with Asparagus, Glazed Brie and Creamed Leek. Their prices are also surprisingly affordable for a fine dining restaurant.

Chapter 5:
Accommodation

Finding a place to stay in Scotland is hard. And that is only because you're literally spoiled with choices. You'll certainly find your fair share of traditional hotels, hostels, B & B's and resorts, but if you want to take it up a notch, you can even find remote lighthouses, yurts, tipis or even converted churches in which to spend the night. The good news is that accommodations in Scotland can generally fit a variety of budget ranges.

Live in the lap of luxury in Scotland's lavish resorts

Gleneagles Hotel

First established in 1924, Gleneagles Hotel was once described as an absolute "Riviera in the Highlands." This truly breathtaking countryside estate is so opulent that it even made it onto the list of the 'Leading Hotels of the World.' With a restaurant that holds two Michelin stars, an award-winning spa and 3-championship golf courses, the Gleneagles Hotel also offers a series of traditionally Scottish activities such as wildlife photography, pitch and putt, snooker, fishing, archery, cycling, falconry, off-road driving and horseback riding. With stunningly elegant rooms and suites that overlook the vivid green grounds, this hotel also features several cafes and restaurants.

The Balmoral

No, this is not the Balmoral Castle where the royals escape to every year. But it's most likely just as grand. With seamless glamor and elegance, this hotel stands as a landmark in Edinburgh. Whether you want a traditional Scottish afternoon tea or to simply sip on drinks in their whiskey bar, you can be sure that there's always plenty to do at the Balmoral. Other activities include distillery tours, highland games, luxury yacht hires and even ghost hunting in one of Scotland's oldest castles.

Guests can choose between different types of suites, deluxe, executive or classic rooms that echo the same lavish opulence that fills the rest of the hotel. I have to say that I quite enjoyed the four different spas: Forte Health, Forte Nourish, Forte Fitness and Forte Rituals, among others. Each spa features strong local accents and all are guaranteed to revitalize and reenergize you so you can properly enjoy the rest of your vacation.

Comlongon Castle Hotel

Here's your chance to actually sleep in a century-old Scottish castle! Set on over 120 acres of woodlands, with a carp pond, manicured gardens, and sweeping lawns and lakes, this particular hotel is brimming with timeless elegance and luxury. Guests even get to choose between 14 different suites, each of them bearing an individual theme. All the rooms are decked in traditional Scottish architecture, including massive poster beds with the occasional touch of tartan. In fact, if you've just gotten married, you can even go for the private Honeymoon Lodge which stands detached from the main castle.

If you ask me, the castle's location only adds to its convenience. The Comlongon Castle is actually a mere two hours away from Glasgow and Edinburgh, and 20 minutes from Carlisle. Especially suited to people travelling between Scotland and England (it's just across the Scottish border), this castle offers bespoke services to ensure that you're pampered during the entire duration of your stay.

Mid-range and family accommodation in Scotland

Hotel Travelodge Dumbarton

If you're travelling with your family or are otherwise on a limited budget, you can check out the Hotel Travelodge Dumbarton. Located 2.59km from the city center and 18.17km from the train station, this particular lodge offers parking services and comfortable accommodations that can easily suit solo travelers or couples, as well as families. Guests can choose between spacious single, double, triple or quadruple rooms, and pets are welcome.

Holiday Inn Express Inverness

Not far from some of the major Scottish attractions in Inverness is the Holiday Inn Express. This mid-range hotel even offers a traditional buffet breakfast as well as a lounge that offers different types of specialty drinks. Alternatively, guests can also head off to the nearby restaurants or simply ask for the hotel staff to order their take-out meals. While it is quite budget-friendly, the hotel even offers professional meeting rooms, dry cleaning services, and free on-site parking, as well as irons and ironing boards in the bedrooms. You can choose between twin, double, family or accessible rooms.

Highlander Inn Hotel and Whiskey Bar

My personal favorite, the Highlander Inn Hotel and Whiskey Bar is exceptionally cozy in spite of its budget-friendly price. Ideal for anyone who wants to enjoy a quiet retreat, this inn hotel only has 8 bedrooms in the main building, ensuring that you benefit from a personalized service. Rooms are decked out in warm reds and beiges, echoing the hearty earthiness of Scotland. In the evening, you can head over to the on-site whiskey bar which offers an extended array of drinks. Don't judge me, but what I loved the most about this hotel inn was its 'Unique Whiskey Breakfast,' which includes a choice of cereal, orange juice, haggis, black pudding, tea, coffee, toast and—believe it or not—a whole dram of Oishii Whisky. Now that's what I call an excellent start to the day!

Check out some more adventurous options

One of the interesting things about Scotland is that you don't necessarily need to opt for a conventional hotel or hostel. This is the country that offers so much more in terms of accommodation, such as the following.

Ben Lomond Yurts

Located in Stirling, these yurts will literally make you feel like you're one with the Scottish wilderness. Designed for an exquisitely homey and earthly feel, and crafted from locally-sourced materials, the Ben Lomond Yurts even feature wood-burning stoves, felt wall-hangings, sleepover mats, a double futon and even a double bed. A boardwalk connects the yurts and leads up to a communal kitchen which is perfectly equipped with everything that you'll need to prepare your own meals.

Old Churches House Hotel

This church-turned-hotel is found in the heart of Dunblane and offers surprisingly comfortable accommodations considering that it was once a publicly owned building. Exceptionally charming, with rock walls and an old-fashioned ceiling, this house hotel somehow managed to retain its original charm. All of the bedrooms are equipped with an en-suite bathroom that includes both an old-fashioned washbasin and a contemporary shower. It may be an old building, but free WiFi is available throughout. Facilities include locally sourced breakfast with home-baked bread and all the typical Scottish fixings, as well as various types of beauty treatments and massages in the on-site spa.

Willow Treehouse

Here is your chance to go right back into childhood! Rest assured that the Willow Treehouse is not only entirely suitable for adults, but it was also far more comfortable than I'd anticipated. Within walking distance to the beach, this treehouse stands 2 meters above the ground, offering striking views of the surroundings. What I liked the most about this treehouse was how easily it blended fun and luxury, with a boat-style dining table that swings right down from the wall. On the lower deck, you'll also find swings, love seats and a hammock. More importantly, a bathroom, complete with a hot shower is included on the main story.

Thomas Leon

Chapter 6: Shopping, Scottish Style

There's nothing quite like shopping in Scotland. Forget about tacky souvenirs and poor-quality overpriced clothes and accessories. One of the things that I liked the most about shopping in Scotland was the exceptional quality available. There was something really elegant about their souvenirs as well. Instead of the typical endless rows of plastic coasters, Scottish souvenirs were all about rich pewters, glass and crystals.

Take it from me, this is the country to shop in if you'd like to get your hands on some of the highest-quality items in the world.

Clothes, candies and more

While you can shop for souvenirs in basically any corner of Scotland, I would suggest that you go souvenir hunting in Glasgow or Edinburg. From my experience, shopping can be quite expensive in Scotland, so be sure to hunt around for bargains and try to favor markets over lavish shopping malls if you're trying to watch your budget. If you do feel like splurging, however, rest assured that the capital is bursting with high-end malls, luxury brands, high street and designer items. According to the locals, the beautiful scenery in Scotland inspired craftsmen to create unique sculptures, Harris Tweed and handmade jewelry which you can take home.

If—like me—you happen to be a shopaholic, rest assured that the streets of Scotland are full of art galleries, countryside farms, harbors and quaint little shops in which you can actually haggle the price. Whether you want to pick up a few treats for yourself, or bring back gifts for your friends and family, you can be sure that you'll find something in just about any corner of Scotland. In fact, this country also has its fair share of farmer's markets where you can acquire different types of vintage clothes, handcrafted soaps, decorative tubes or pots of Barley sugar. I was lucky enough to get my hands on Scottish candy such as sugar free Boilings, Moo Fee chocolates, Raspberry macaroon and Sweet Butter tablets.

Scottish Souvenirs

Here are some of my favorite traditional souvenirs from Scotland.

Quaich

A small silver drinking bowl that feature a Celtic design. While most models are available in silver, quaichs are also made from glass, wood, brass, horn, pewter and even stone. Depending on the material used, these drinking bowls can cost between $20 and $200.

Malt Scotch Whiskey

Since Scotland is known for its quality scotch and whiskey, it shouldn't come as a surprise that most shops and distilleries offer gift boxes that capture the exclusiveness and rarity of Scottish beverages. I personally headed back home with a couple of Single Malt Scotch Whiskey which is made from malted barley. This bottle is securely packed in a box but I would still recommend that you wrap it up in bubble wrap if you're flying back home. Prices range between $20 and $340.

Kilts

Come on. You can't leave Scotland without at least one kilt in your suitcase now, can you? The mark of a true, virile and strong Scotsman, kilts are globally acclaimed for their vivid red tartan print and thick heavy fabric. A nod to the rich Scottish culture, kilts are also considered to be symbols of patriotism for the locals. Depending on the quality, you can expect to spend between $40 and $450 for a kilt.

Edinburgh Crystal

If you're looking for luxury souvenirs to bring back home, head over to the capital where you'll be able to get your hands on the world-famous Edinburgh Crystal in different sizes and forms. Examples include crystal bells, baskets, bowls, decanters and drinking glasses. Available in John Lewis, those crystal pieces can be expensive but it's actually considered as an investment. Just be sure to let the staff know that you'll be flying so they can pack it up with extra bubble wrap and add different layers to protect your purchases. Do expect to spend between $100 and $400.

Knits, Tweeds and Cashmere

In Glasgow, you can expect to get your hands on traditionally Scottish fabrics. Brands such as Harris Tweed are iconic to Scotland and offer various types of high-quality items such as knitwear, tweed camera bags and even cashmere socks, among others. Prices can range between $20 and $300. If you're visiting Scotland during the sales season, I would certainly suggest that you invest in some good-quality Scottish tweed. Not only is this one of the warmest fabrics you can find, but tweed and knits have been known to last for a lifetime, providing you with an excellent investment from Scotland.

Conclusion

With centuries of folklore, ancient monuments, legendary myths and a plethora of unearthed gems to its name, it should come as no surprise that Scotland is an exceptionally popular tourist destination that attracts millions of visitors per year. And while one might assume that the place would be packed with visitors, this couldn't be further from the truth. In fact, the only places that felt crowded to me were those popular Edinburg pubs on Friday nights. Scotland is actually so immense that you'd be hard-pressed to find packs of noisy and overly-ebullient tourists ruining your fun. Most of the time, it's the solitude that hits you, especially in the remote countryside

The Scottish wilderness coupled with the truly majestic weather combines beautifully to create an almost out-of-this-world experience. With the kind of greenery unlike anything I'd ever seen before, Scotland certainly does offer something for just about anyone. So, grab your glass of malt whiskey and draw in that gloriously pure air as you soak in the very best that Scotland has to offer.

Thank you so much for reading this book. I know there are many choices out there for travel books, so I'm really grateful that you picked up this book.

I hope this book is useful for you.

If you like the book, would you please do me a huge favor and write me a review on Amazon?

Your review is really important to me and it helps me feel confident writing more travel books.

I would really appreciate it and look forward to reading your review.

Thank you so much!

Thomas

Check out my other travel books...

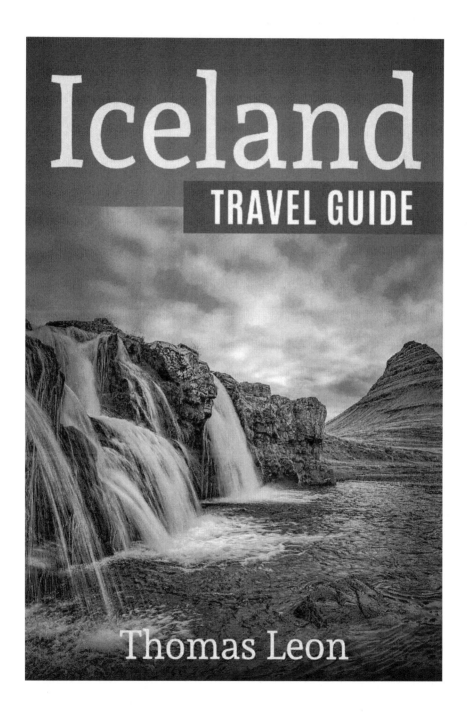

Iceland
TRAVEL GUIDE

Thomas Leon

CUBA

TRAVEL GUIDE

Thomas Leon

Hawaii
TRAVEL GUIDE

Thomas Leon

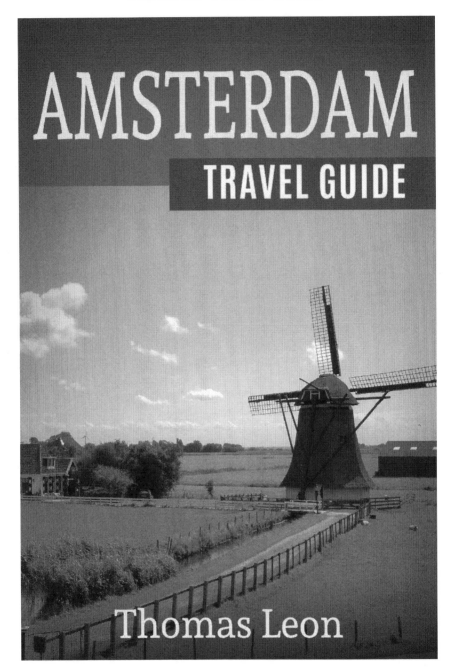

AMSTERDAM
TRAVEL GUIDE

Thomas Leon

Thomas Leon

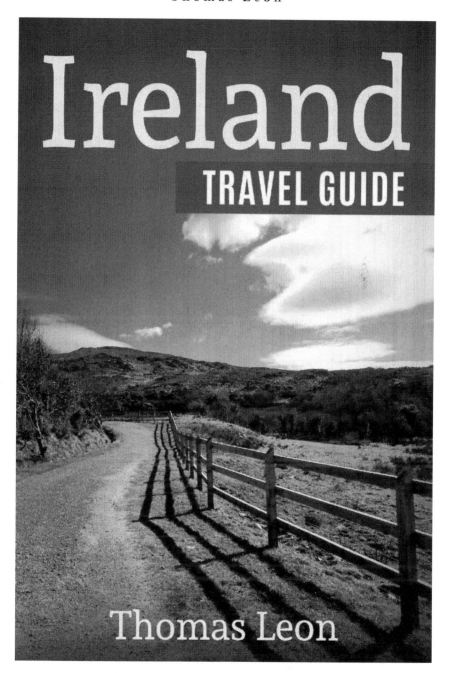

Made in the USA
Middletown, DE
26 February 2018